Sea Creatures

CD-ROM and Book

DOVER PUBLICATIONS, INC.
Mineola, New York

The CD-ROM on the inside back cover contains all of the images shown in the book. Each image has been scanned at 300 dpi and saved in TIFF format. There is no installation necessary. Just insert the CD into your computer and call the images into your favorite software (refer to the documentation with your software for further instructions).

All of the graphics files are in the Images folder on the CD. Every image has a unique file name in the following format: xxx.TIF. The first 3 digits of the file name correspond to the number printed under the image in the book. The last 3 letters of the file name, "TIF," refer to the file format. So, 001.TIF would be the first file in the Images folder.

Also included on the CD-ROM is Dover Design Manager, a simple graphics editing program for Windows, that will allow you to view, print, crop, and rotate the images.

For technical support, contact:
Telephone: 1 (617) 249-0245
Fax: 1 (617) 249-0245
Email: dover@artimaging.com
Internet: **http://www.dovertechsupport.com**
The fastest way to receive technical support is via email or the Internet.

Bibliographical Note

Sea Creatures CD-ROM and Book first published by Dover Publications, Inc., in 2005, is a new selection of designs from Albertus Seba's *Locupletissimi rerum naturalium thesauri accurata descriptio.* 4 vols. Amsterdam. 1734–1765.

Dover Full-Color Electronic Design Series®

International Standard Book Number: 0-486-99666-2

Manufactured in the United States of America
Dover Publications, Inc., 31 East 2nd Street, Mineola, N.Y. 11501

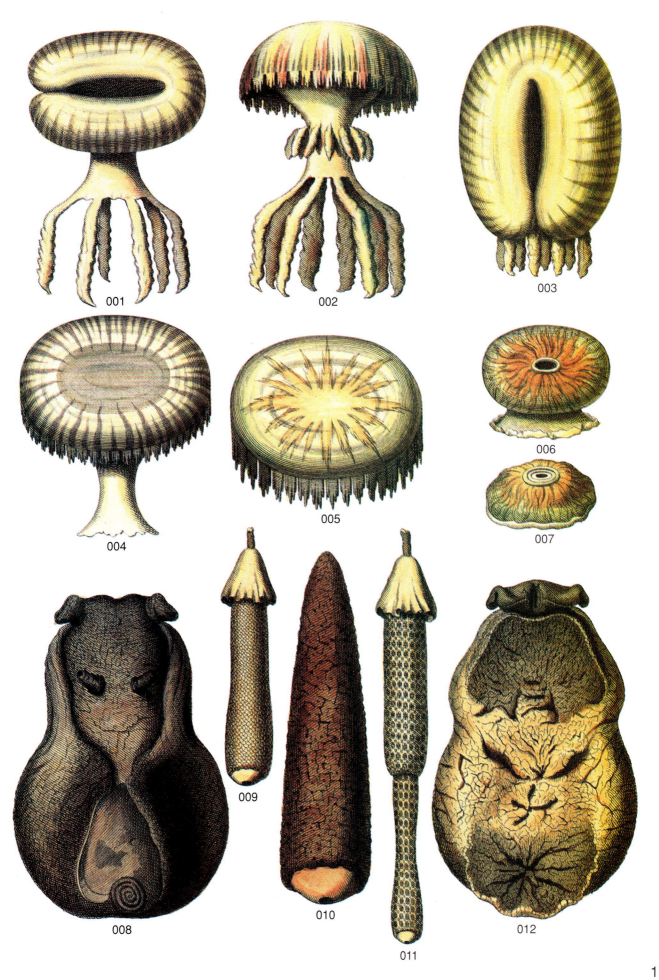

001

002

003

004

005

006

007

008

009

010

011

012

1

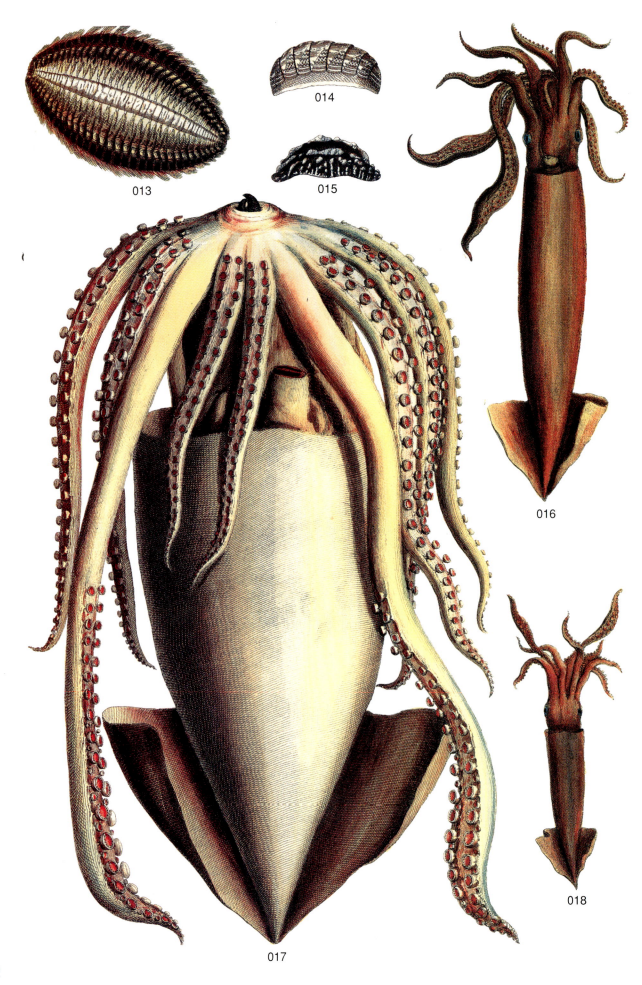

013

014

015

016

017

018

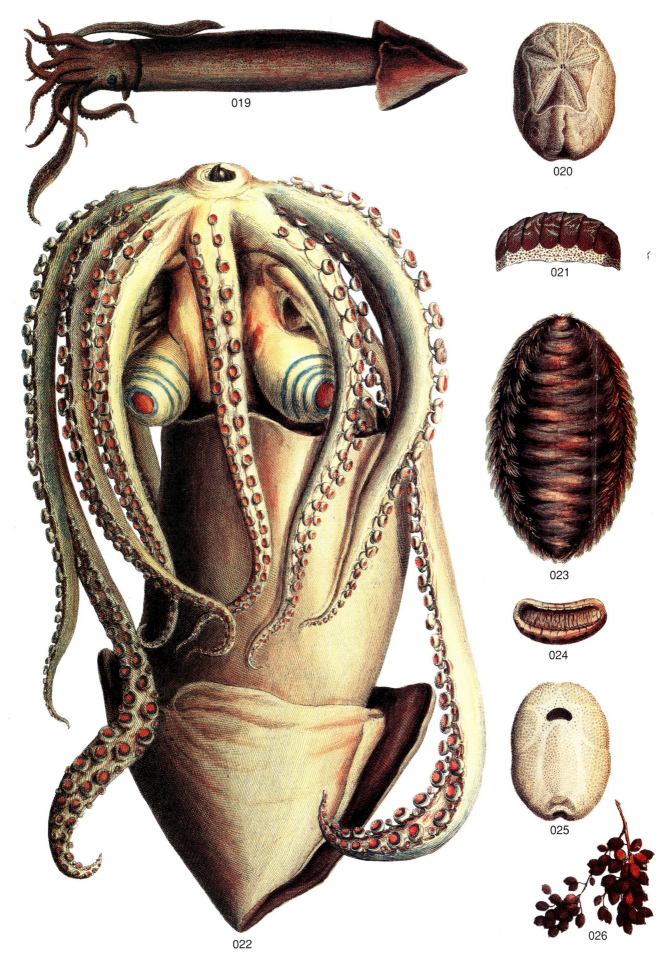

019

020

021

022

023

024

025

026

027

028

029

030

031

032

033

034

035

036

037

038

039

040

041

042

043

044

045

046

047

048

049

050

051

052

053

054

055

056

057

058

059

060

061

062

063

064

065

066

067

068

069

070

071

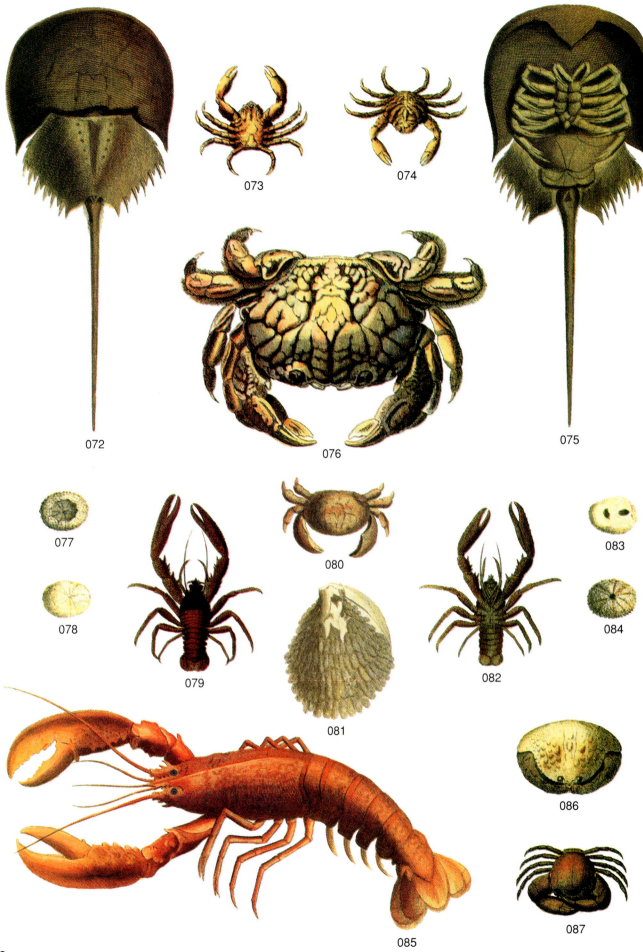

072

073

074

075

076

077

078

079

080

081

082

083

084

085

086

087

8

088 089 090 001 092 093

094 095 096 097 098 099

102

103

100 101 104 105

108

106 107 109 110

111

112 113 114 116 117

115

118 119 120 121

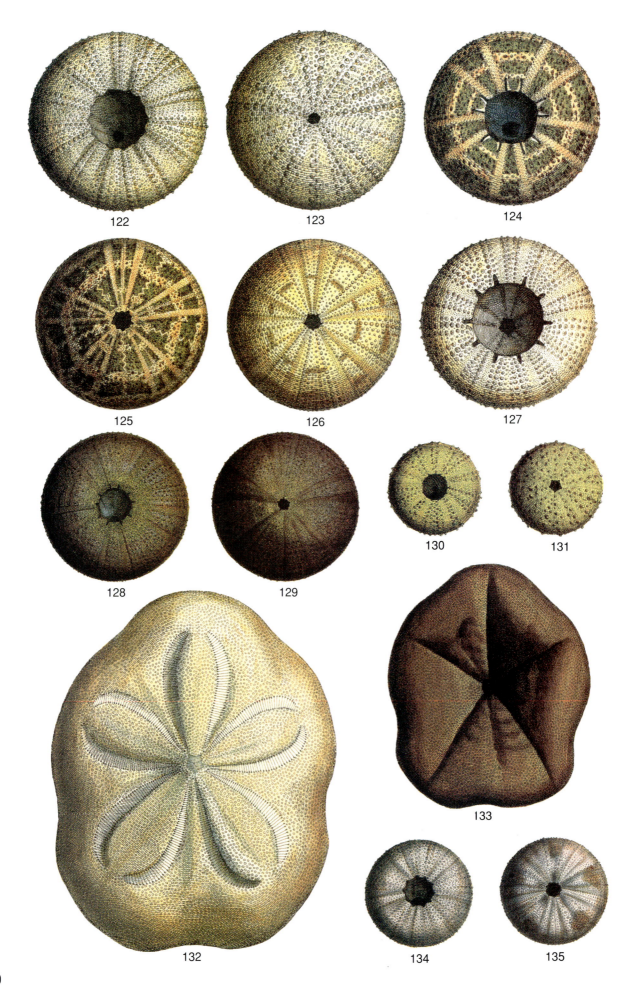

122

123

124

125

126

127

128

129

130

131

132

133

134

135

136

137

138

139

140

141

142

143

144

145

146

147

11

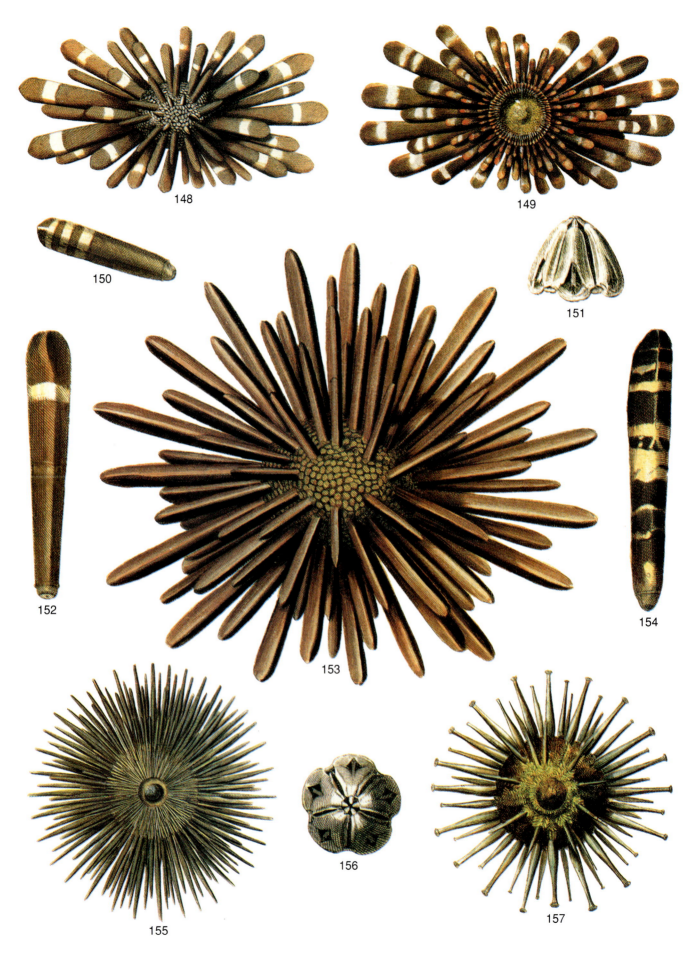

148

149

150

151

152

153

154

155

156

157

12

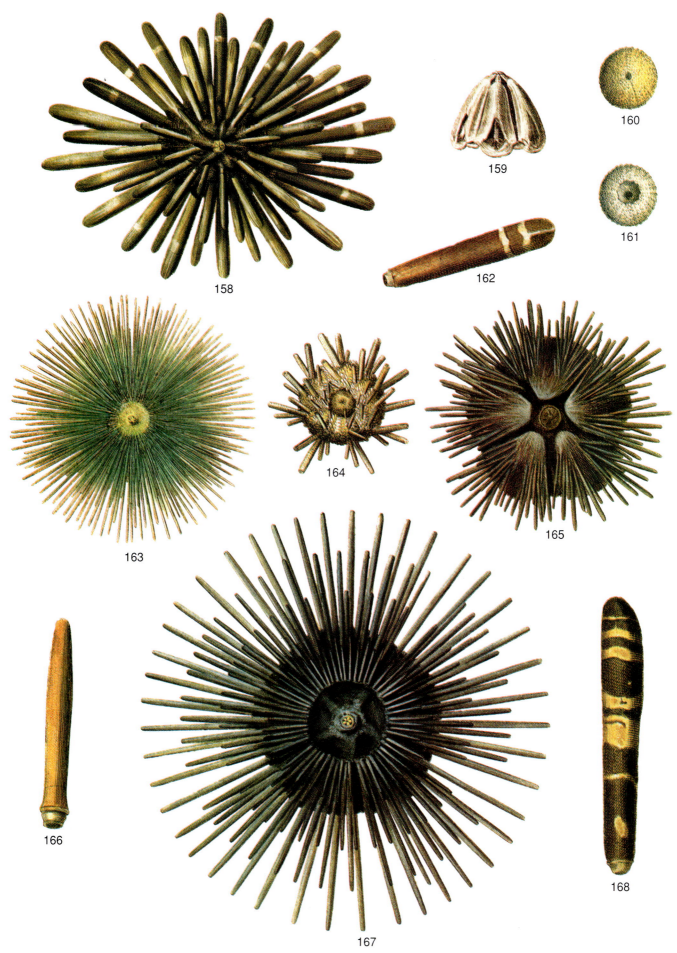

158

159

160

161

162

163

164

165

166

167

168

13

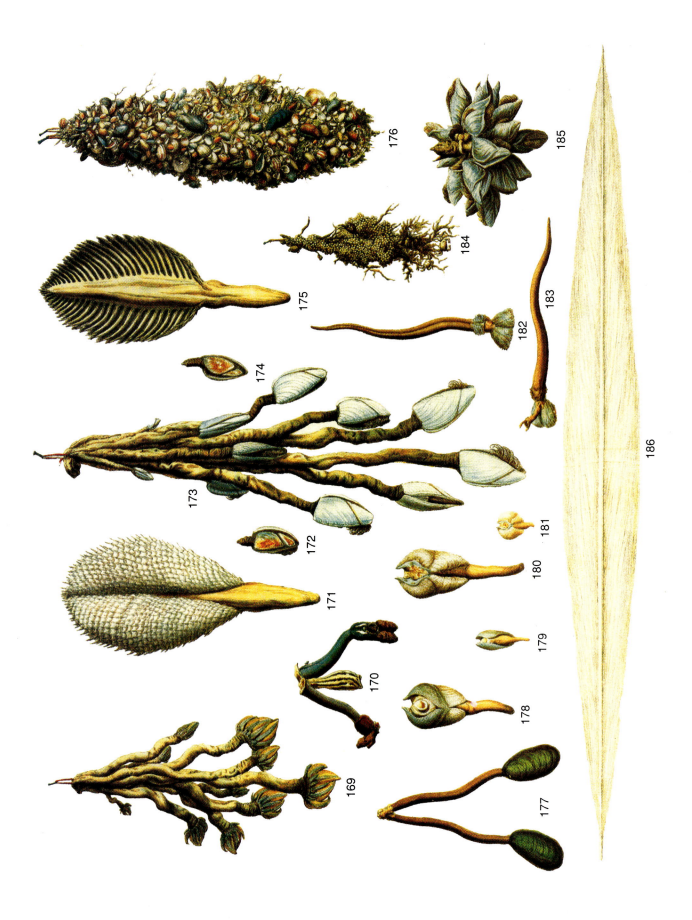

176

185

184

175

183

182

174

186

173

181

172

180

171

179

170

178

169

177

14

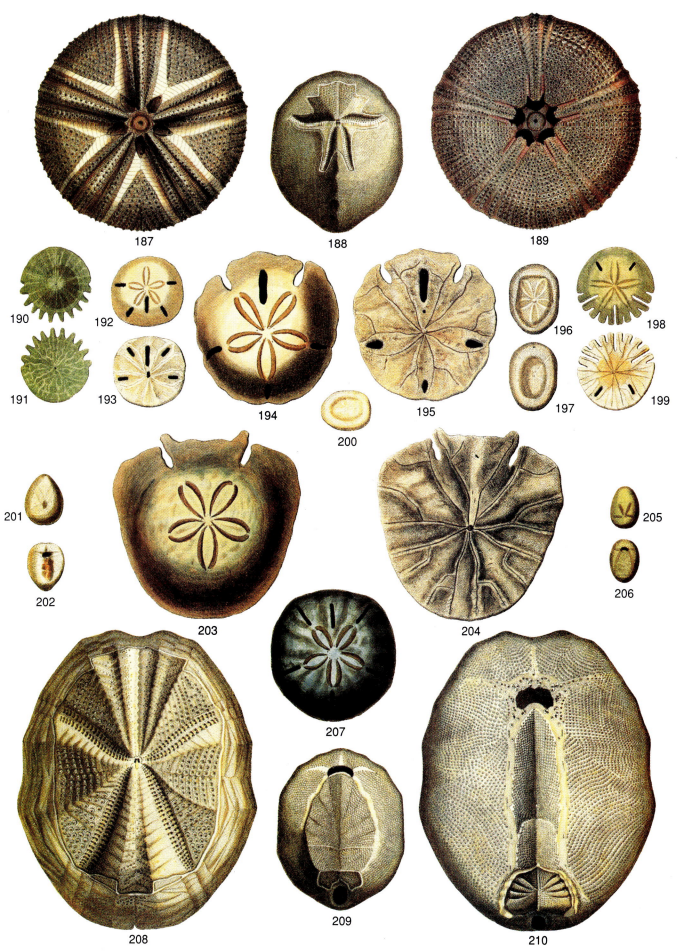

211

212

213

214

215

216

217

218

219

220

221

222

223

224

225

226

227

228

229

230

231

232

233

234

236

237

238

239

240

241

242

243

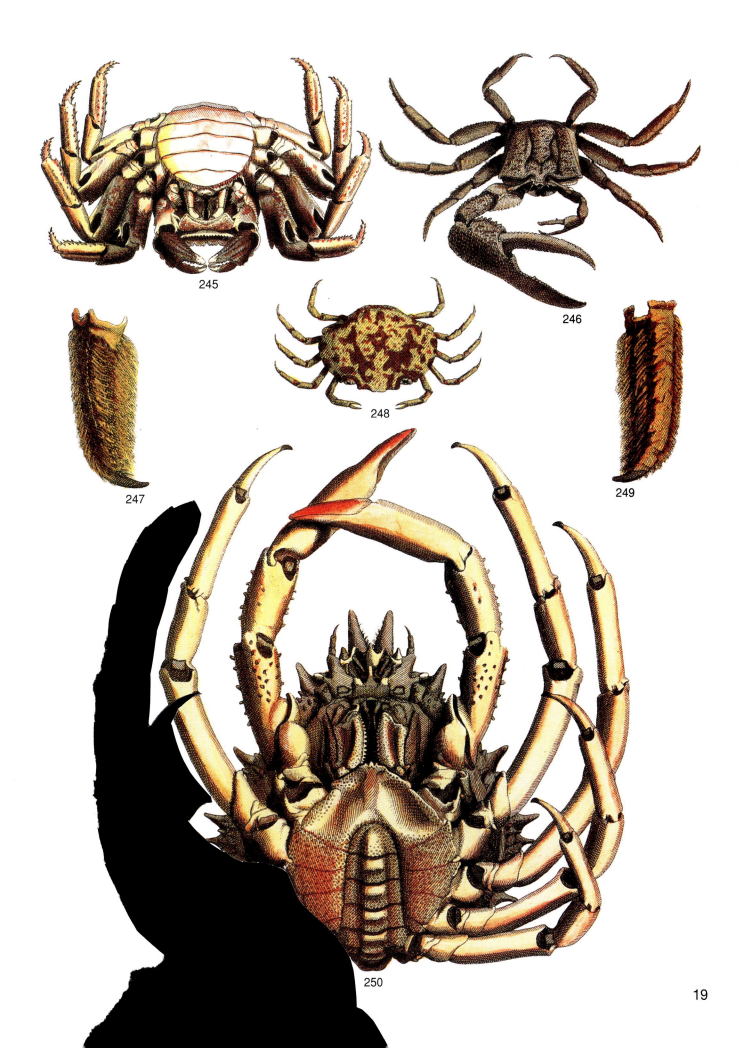

245

246

247

248

249

250

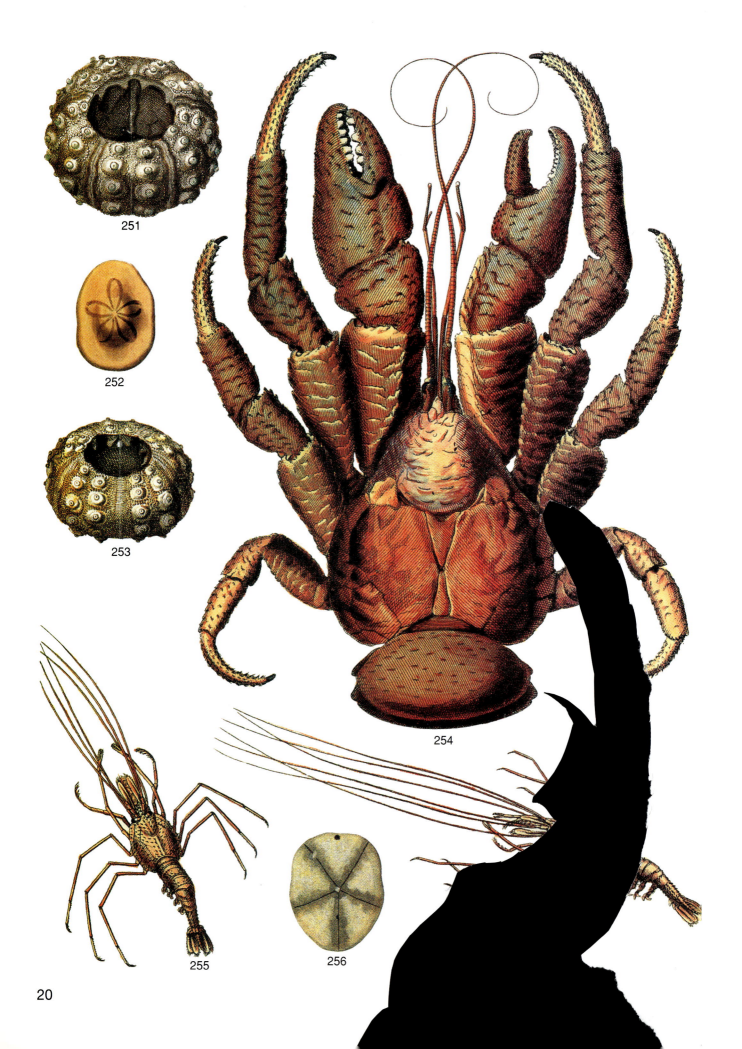

251

252

253

254

255

256

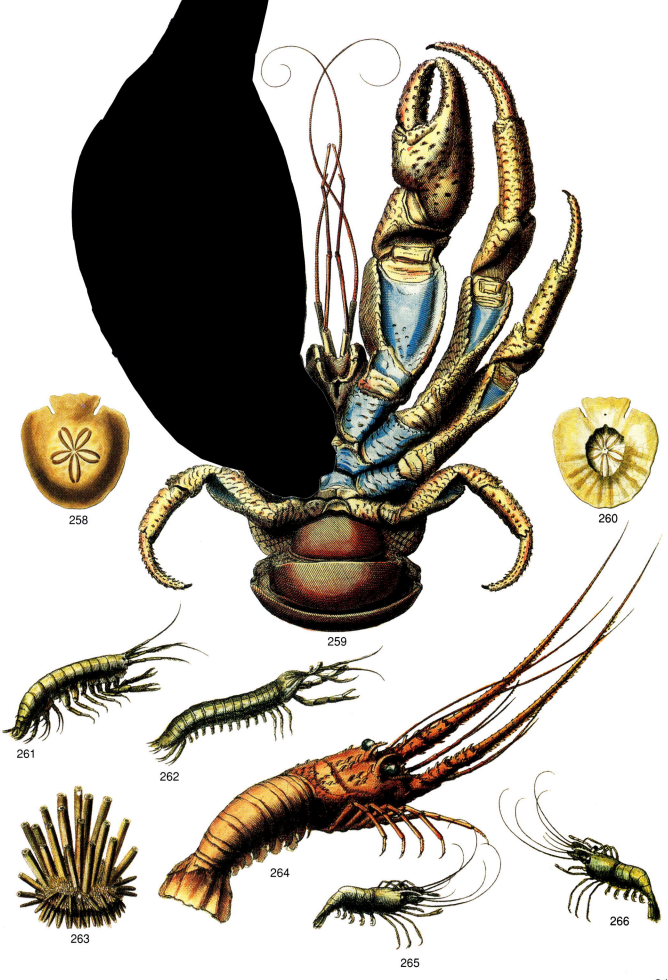

258

259

260

261

262

263

264

265

266

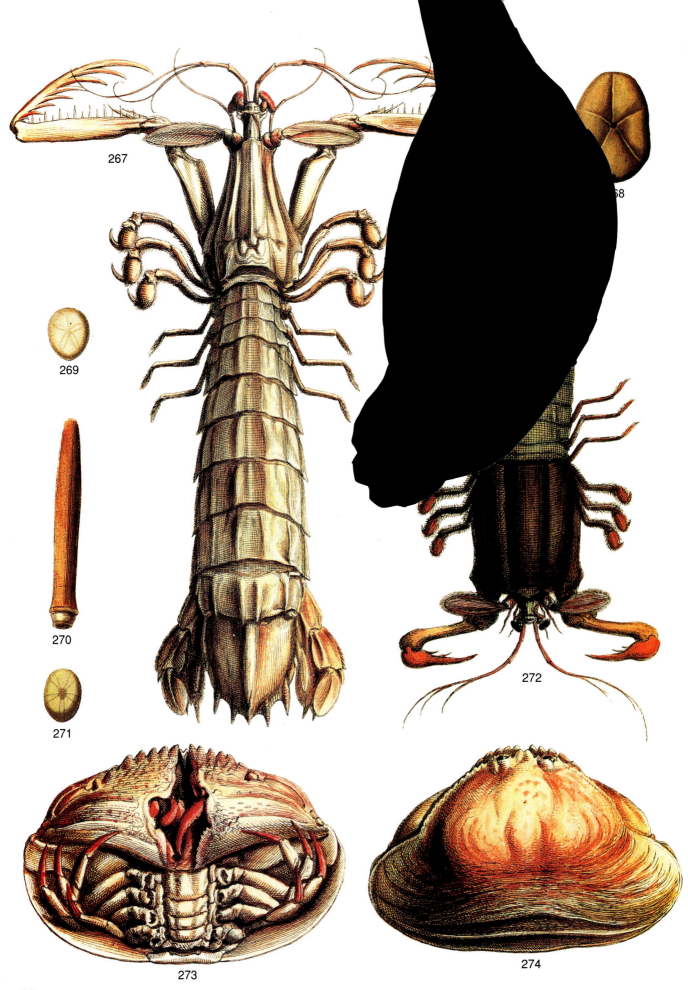

267

268

269

270

271

272

273

274

275

276

278

277

279

280

281

282

283

23

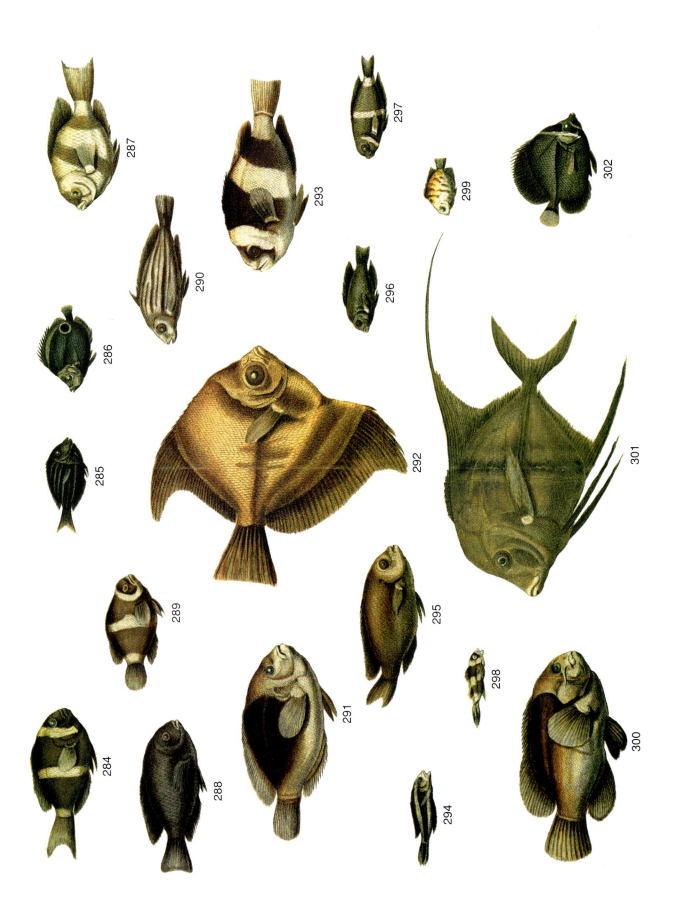

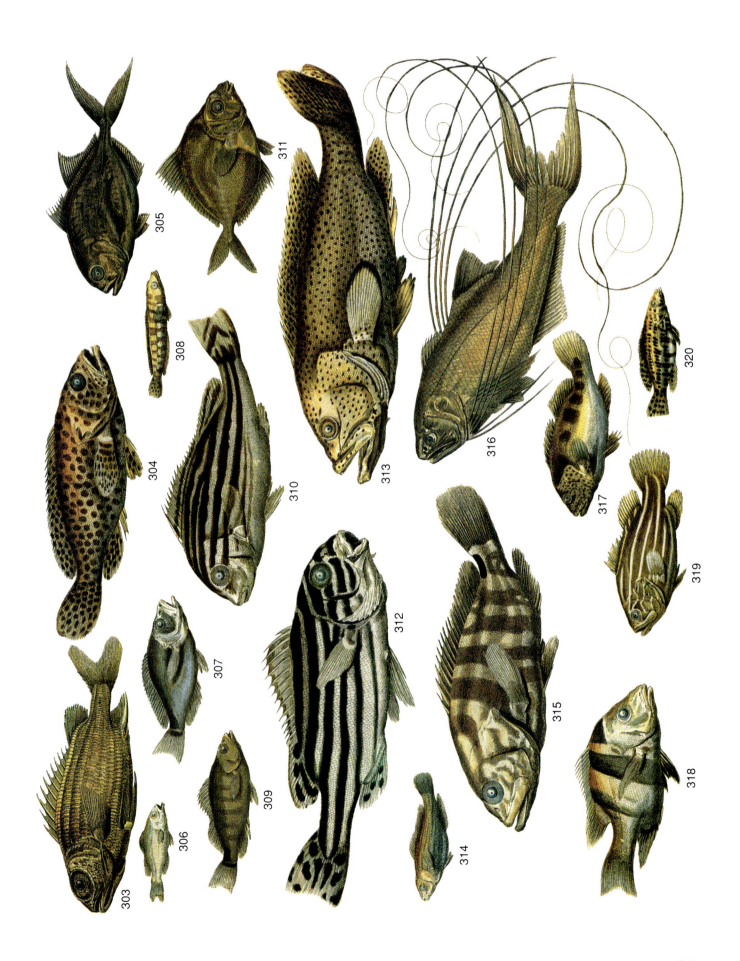

303

304

305

306

307

308

309

310

311

312

313

314

315

316

317

318

319

320

321

322

323

324

325

326

327

328

329

330

331

332

333

334

335

336

337

338

339

340

341

342

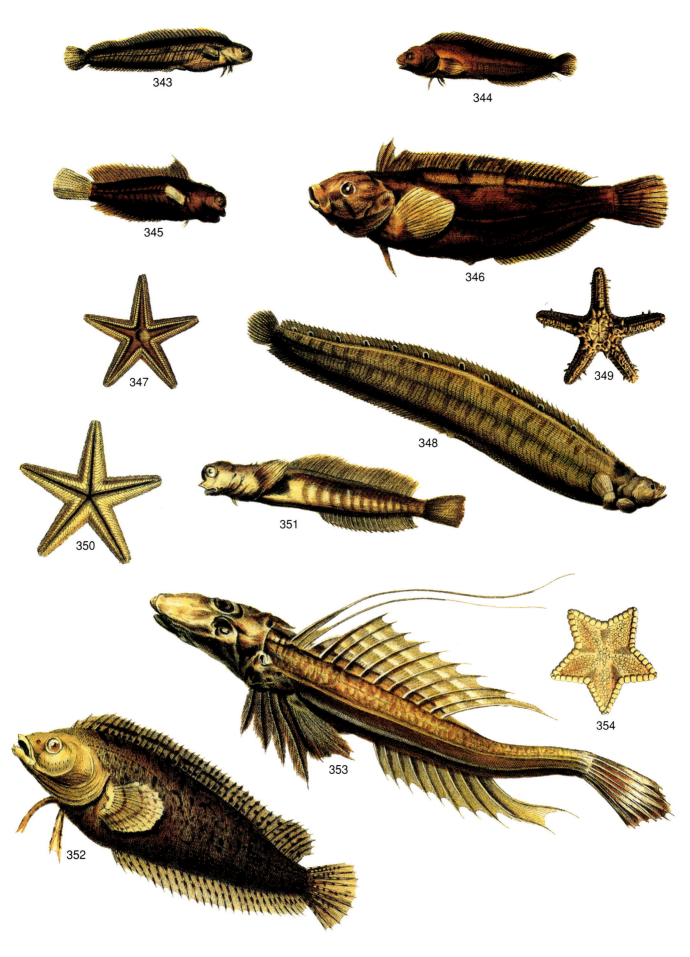

343

344

345

346

347

348

349

350

351

352

353

354

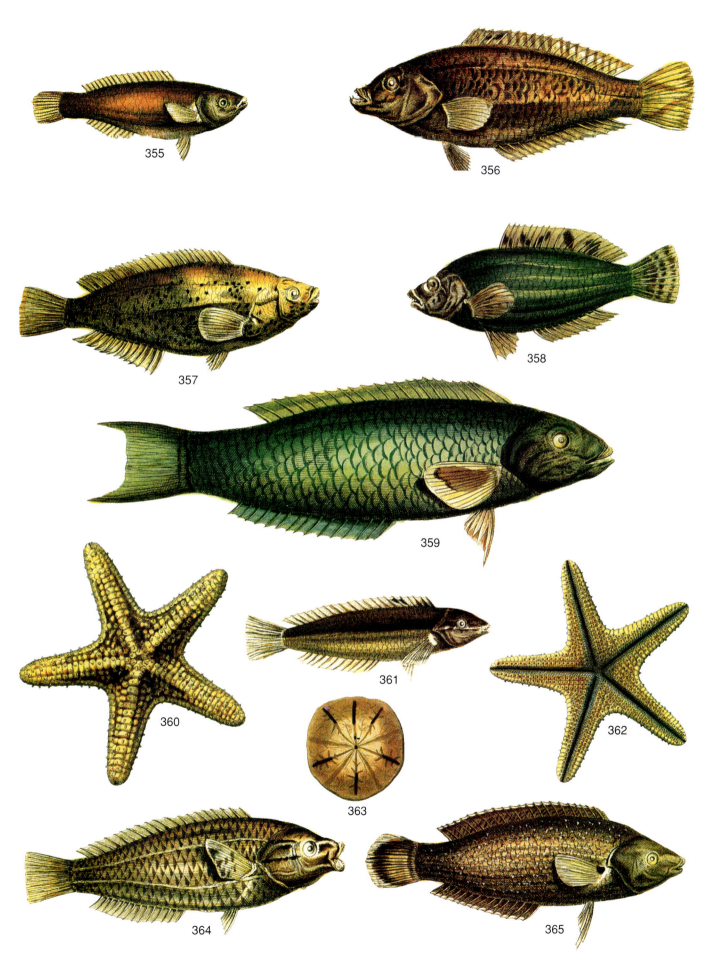

355

356

357

358

359

360

361

362

363

364

365

29

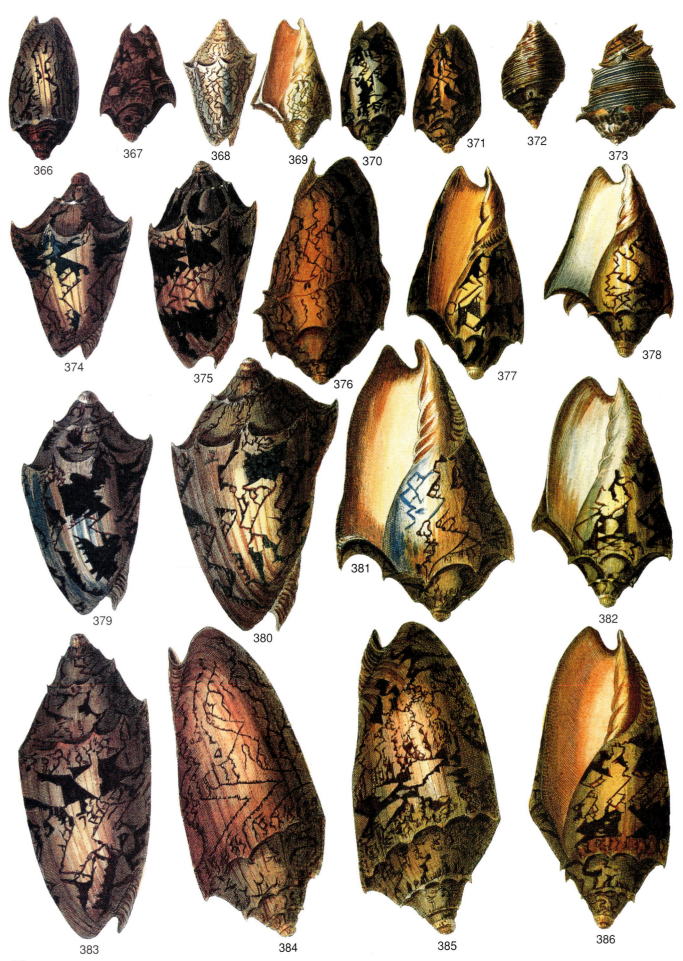

366
367
368
369
370
371
372
373
374
375
376
377
378
379
380
381
382
383
384
385
386

30

387

388

389

390

391

392

393

394

395

396

397

398

399

400

401

402

403

404

405

406

407

408

409

410

411

412

413

414

415

416

417

418

419

420

421

422

423

424

425

426

427

428

429

430

431

432

433

434

435

436

437

438

439

440

441

442

443

444

445

446

447

448

33

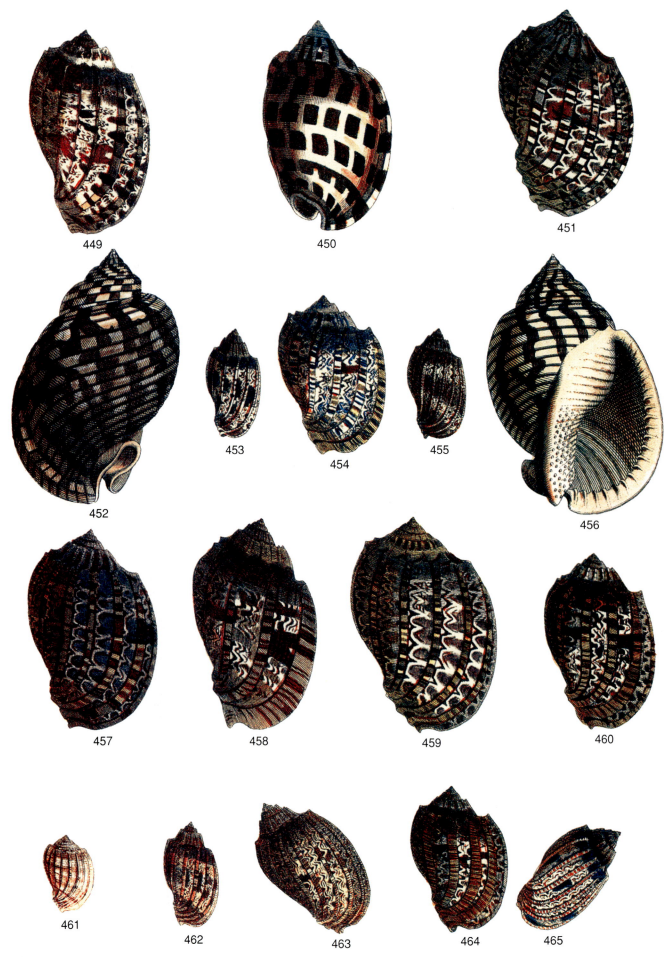

449

450

451

452

453

454

455

456

457

458

459

460

461

462

463

464

465

466

467

468

469

470

471

472

473

474

475

476

477

478

479

35

480

481

483

482

484

485

486

487

488

489

490

491

492

493

494

495

496

497

498

499

500

501

502

503

504

505

506

507

508

509

510

511

512

513

543

544

545

546

561

564

560

563

559

562

558

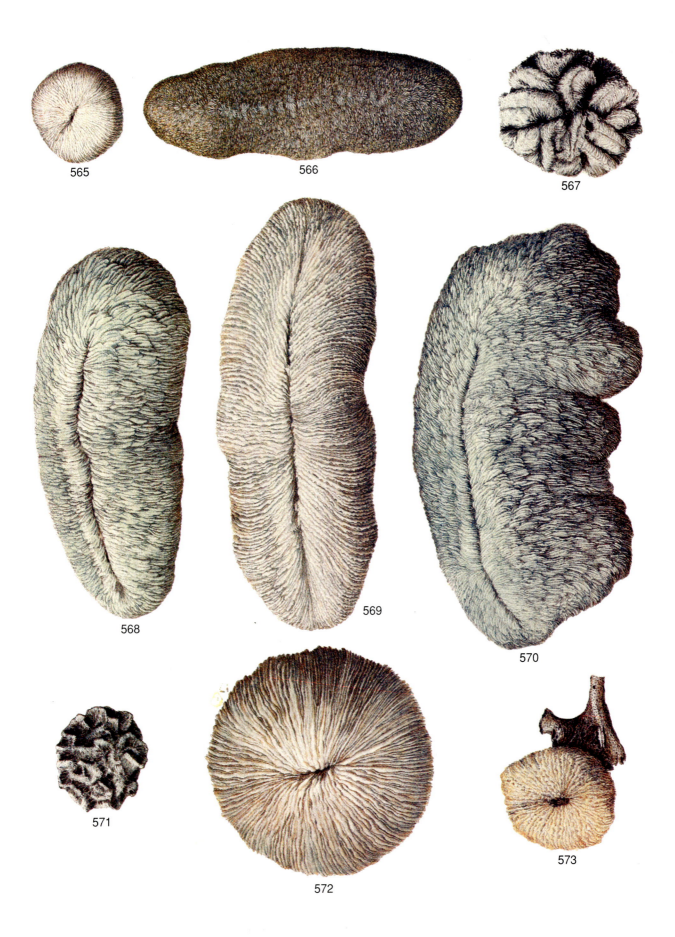

574

575

576

577

578

579

580

581

582

583

Index